Symmetry Crafts

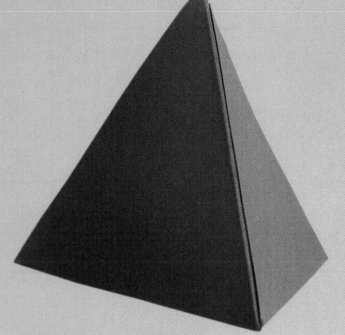

By Amy Houts

CELEBRATION PRESS
Pearson Learning Group

Contents

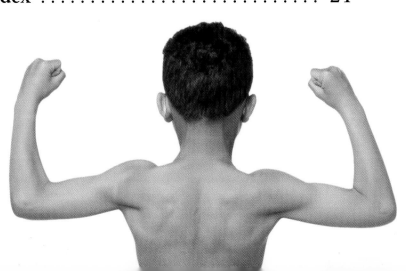

What Is Symmetry?

Did you ever see a tree reflected in water? Did you ever make a greeting card by folding a paper rectangle in half? Did you ever make a design in which one side matched the other? If you have, then you know what **symmetry** is.

A shape has symmetry when the parts on both sides of the shape's center line match. Each half is **congruent**, or matches the other in size and shape. You can see symmetry all around—in plants, animals, buildings, and many objects.

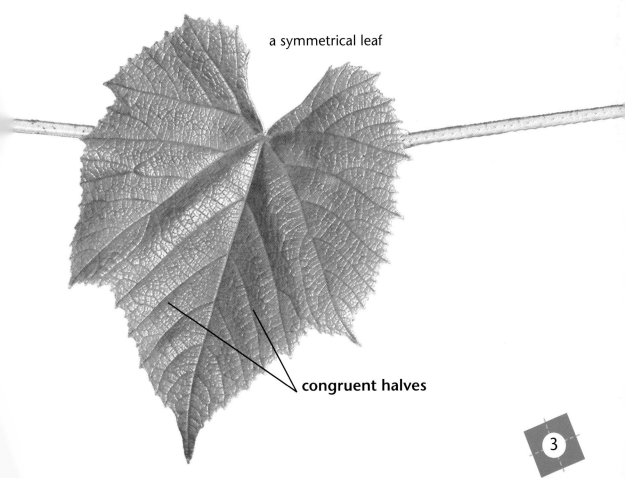

a symmetrical leaf

congruent halves

Symmetry can take different forms. An object with symmetry of **reflection** has two sides. Each side is a mirror image of the other.

The right half of this building, the Taj Mahal in India, is a mirror image of the left half.

Rotation involves turning an object around a center point. If the object has exactly the same appearance when it is rotated, it has rotational symmetry.

If you turn or rotate this starfish, its appearance stays the same.

Translation occurs when you move a shape from one place to another. This simple form of symmetry is often found in artwork.

Now that you know all about symmetry, get ready to make some fun symmetry crafts!

tiles showing translational symmetry

Symmetry Crafts With Reflection

A butterfly can be symmetrical. Imagine a line dividing this butterfly into two halves. The left half is a mirror image, or a reflection, of the right half. You can make a paper butterfly that shows symmetry of reflection.

A butterfly can show symmetry of reflection.

Make a Butterfly

MATERIALS

- 5 pieces of colored paper: yellow, black, purple, blue, orange
- chalk
- scissors
- paste or glue stick

1 Decide on a color for your butterfly wings. Fold the piece of paper in half. Starting at the fold, draw one wing.

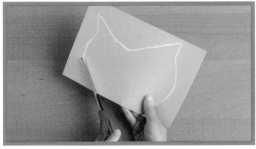

2 Cut on the lines.

3 Unfold the wings.

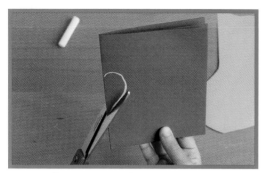

4 Choose another color. Fold the paper in half lengthwise and then in half crosswise. Draw a shape next to the fold, and cut through all the thicknesses. Unfold the shape to see two symmetrical shapes.

5 Arrange the shapes on the butterfly wings so the two sides mirror each other. Paste the shapes on the wings. Repeat with other colors and shapes.

6 Fold a black piece of paper, and draw the body, head, and antennae of the butterfly on the fold. Cut and paste to the center.

Make a Name Design

Did you ever see trees reflected in a pond? The pond acts like a mirror. This is an example of symmetry of reflection.

You can use symmetry of reflection to make a mirror image of your name. The mirror images will be symmetrical.

1 Fold the paper in half lengthwise.

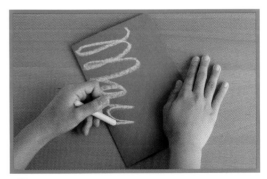

2 Using chalk, write or print your name next to the fold. Make large, thick letters so that you can cut around them. Don't write below the fold.

3 Keeping the paper folded, cut around your name.

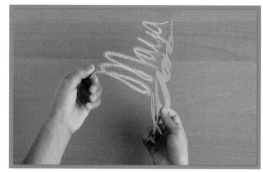

4 Unfold your name.

5 Choose a contrasting color of paper, and glue your name in the center.

Symmetry Crafts With Rotation

Symmetry of rotation can be found in nature. People use it, too. The wings of maple seeds help the seeds rotate in the wind so they can fly to spots where they can grow. The wind turning windmills can generate power for electricity.

A pinwheel is like a windmill or a maple seed. The pinhead is the center point. The pinwheel spins around the pinhead, showing symmetry of rotation. When you rotate, or turn, your pinwheel, the outline is the same.

Maple seeds twirl like pinwheels when they fall to the ground.

A pinwheel looks like a windmill.

Make a Spinning Pinwheel

MATERIALS

- 2 pieces of colored paper
- 1 straight pin with plastic, colored head
- 1 bead
- 2 pencils; one of them should be unsharpened
- scissors
- ruler

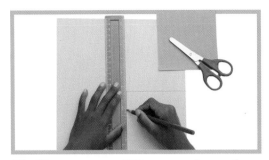

1 Choose two different colors of paper. Measure and draw two 8-by-8-inch squares. Cut them out.

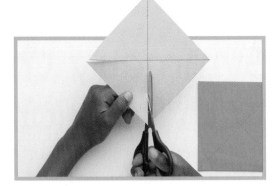

2 Use your ruler to draw two diagonal lines corner to corner across each square. Cut on the lines about two-thirds of the way to the center.

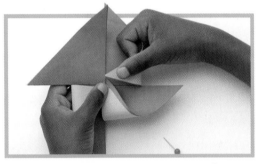

3 Place one square on top of the other. Bend the paper along the cut line, holding down every other corner.

Make sure the pin doesn't stick out of the eraser.

bead

4 Push a pin through the corners of the paper. Thread the pin through the bead and then push it into the eraser of the pencil.

5 Blow on your pinwheel, and watch the rotation.

Make a Tetrahedron

MATERIALS

- colored paper
- pencil and pen
- compass
- ruler
- scissors
- paper clip
- yarn

What is a **tetrahedron**? This **three-dimensional** geometric shape looks like a pyramid. A tetrahedron has four sides, or **faces**. Each side is a triangle. Two faces come together at an **edge**. Edges come together at each **vertex**. If you look down at the top while turning the tetrahedron, you'll see the shape stays the same, showing symmetry of rotation.

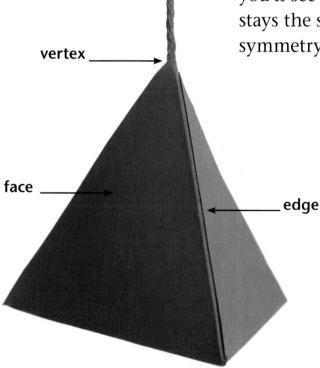

vertex

face

edge

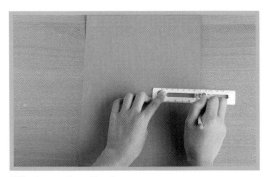

1 A tool called a **compass** will help you measure and draw circles. Using a compass and a pencil, draw a circle.

2 Position the point of your compass anywhere on the outline of the circle. Draw another circle.

position your compass here

3 Position the point of your compass on either of the places where the two circles **intersect**. Draw a third circle.

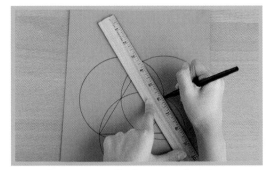

4 Draw small dots at the 5 points where the circles intersect. Use a ruler and a pen to connect each dot to the ones next to it. You will see four triangles.

5 The small areas between the straight lines and the curved lines are called tabs. Mark three of the tabs with an *X* as shown in the photo. (The three tabs to mark are highlighted in yellow.)

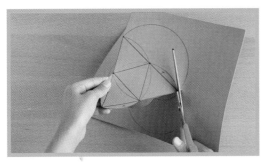

6 Cut out the shape made by the four triangles and the three tabs. (Cut off the tabs that are not marked.) These triangles will become the faces of the tetrahedron.

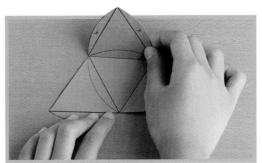

7 Fold the triangles on each line, and press the fold.

8 Glue the tabs to the inside of the triangles. There will be one triangle without tabs.

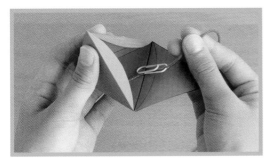

9 Tie a length of yarn to a paper clip. Place the paper clip inside the tetrahedron. Then, glue the last edge.

Make a Picture Stand

You can use a tetrahedron to make a stand to display a photograph or a drawing. Like the tetrahedron you made, the picture stand is a symmetrical shape that can be rotated. No matter how you rotate, turn, or place the stand, it has the same shape.

MATERIALS

- 6 straws
- 7 rubber bands
- photograph

Shapes in 3-D

There are only five three-dimensional shapes with equal sides, angles, and faces. The tetrahedron, made of four triangles, is one. The cube, made of six squares, is another.

The others are the octahedron, made of 8 triangles; the dodecahedron, made up of 12 pentagons; and the icosahedron, made of 20 triangles.

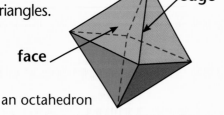

edge

face

an octahedron

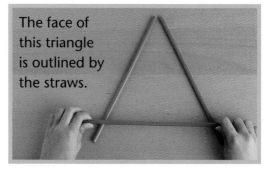

The face of this triangle is outlined by the straws.

1 Use three straws to make a triangle shape. Overlap the ends of the straws.

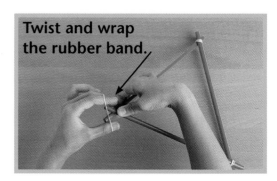

Twist and wrap the rubber band.

2 Wrap a rubber band around each of the three crossed ends of the straws.

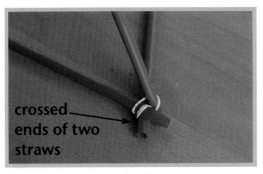

crossed ends of two straws

3 Insert the end of a straw between the crossed ends of two straws. Hold this straw so it is leaning toward the center above the triangle. Wrap another rubber band around the three straw ends.

4 Repeat Step 3 with another straw. Two straws now point toward the center above the triangle.

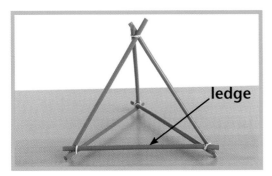

ledge

5 Place the last straw in between the remaining crossed straw ends. Wrap a rubber band around the three crossed ends to connect them. Then, wrap a rubber band around the three straw tops that meet above the triangle.

6 Pull one straw forward to form the ledge of your picture stand. Place a photo on it.

A Symmetry Craft With Translation

You can find many examples of translational symmetry if you look around. Look at a fence or the skin of a pineapple. You'll see the same shape is repeated.

You can make a paper chain to show a translation. A paper chain is a repeating pattern cut from folded paper. The same shapes are repeated in the same **plane**, or level surface.

translational symmetry in a pineapple (left) and honeycomb (right)

Make Action Figures

MATERIALS

- colored paper
- pencil
- scissors
- tape

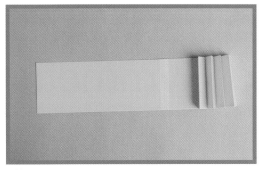

1 Fold a piece of paper in half, lengthwise. Cut the paper along the fold. Then, tape the two strips together to make a long strip.

2 Fold the paper back and forth like an accordion. Make all the folds the same size and wide enough to draw on.

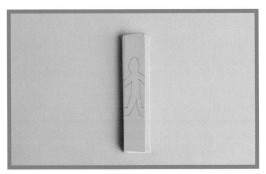

do not cut

3 Use a pencil to draw a person. Make sure the arms and legs are against the fold.

4 Cut through all thicknesses. Do not cut the places without lines.

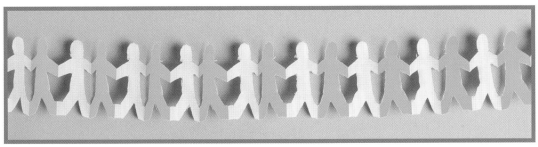

5 Unfold the paper. You'll see a chain of action figures.

Crafts With Lines of Symmetry

Some symmetrical objects, like butterflies and hearts, have one **line of symmetry**. The figure can be folded along the line so that both halves match.

Other objects have more than one line of symmetry. For instance, a square has four. A star has five. A snowflake has six.

Actually, snowflakes show several types of symmetry. If you drew a line down the center of a snowflake, the left and right sides would match. This shows reflection. If you turn a snowflake, the outline is the same. This shows symmetry of rotation. Shapes are also repeated, showing translation.

The snowflake patterns you'll make in the next craft activity can't be found in nature. Why not? Real snowflakes have six sides! The patterns in this craft do, however, have lines of symmetry.

Snowflakes have six sides, or branches.

Make a Snowflake Pattern

1 To make a square, fold an 8½-by-11-inch sheet of paper to line up the top edge with the side edge. Cut.

2 Turn the paper so a corner is at the top, and then fold the paper in half to make a triangle.

3 Fold in half again to make a smaller triangle. Fold in half once more to make an even smaller triangle.

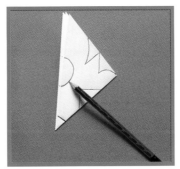

4 Draw shapes on the edges of your triangle.

5 Cut on the lines.

6 Unfold the paper. You made a snowflake pattern!

You can put your snowflake patterns on a string and hang them up.

Make a Kaleidoscope

Many things in nature have beautiful, symmetrical patterns. You can create your own symmetrical patterns by making a kaleidoscope.

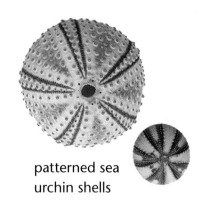

patterned sea urchin shells

Materials:

- mirror board
- pencil
- ruler
- scissors
- tape
- tracing paper
- clear plastic cut from a bag
- transparent beads
- small pieces of colored plastic
- colored paper
- glue stick

1 Measure and cut mirror board, 4½ inches by 8 inches. Measure and score two lines, lengthwise, 1½ inches apart.

2 Fold along the lines, with the mirror inside. Tape the edges. Tape the clear plastic over the end.

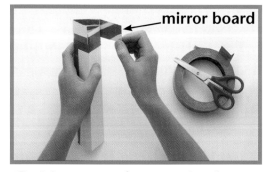

mirror board

3 Measure and cut a strip of mirror board, 4¾ inches by 1½ inches. Tape it around the end of the tube, so that it sticks up over the plastic-covered end.

4 Place the tube upright, with the short piece you added at the top. Drop beads and colored plastic pieces into the tube.

5 Cut a piece of tracing paper in a triangle shape. Tape it over the top of the tube.

How many lines of symmetry do you see in your kaleidoscope patterns?

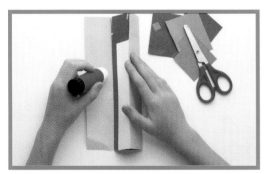

6 Cut a piece of colored paper, 4½ inches by 8 inches. Glue it around the tube.

7 Decorate the tube by cutting and gluing on pieces of colored paper.

8 To use your kaleidoscope, hold the open end near your eye. Face a window or light. Turn the kaledioscope.

Once you understand symmetry, you'll look at the world in a different way. Look around. What types of symmetry do you see: reflection, rotation, or translation? How many lines of symmetry can you count? What you find might inspire you to make up your own symmetry crafts. Have fun!

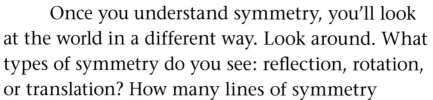

You can find symmetry in many places.

Glossary

compass   an instrument with two hinged legs used for drawing circles

congruent   exactly equal in size and shape

edge   the line formed where two faces come together

faces   flat sides of a three-dimensional shape

intersect   to meet or cross

line of symmetry   the dividing line that separates an object into two matching sides

plane   a level or flat surface

reflection   a type of symmetry that gives a mirror image

rotation   a type of symmetry in which an object has the same outline when turned around a center point

symmetry   an arrangement of parts that gives two matching sides

tetrahedron   a three-dimensional shape with four triangular sides

three-dimensional   having length, width, and depth or height

translation   a type of symmetry in which a shape repeats in the same plane

vertex   a point where two or more edges come together

Index